CAMOUFLAGE
CAROL MUSKE

UNIVERSITY OF PITTSBURGH PRESS

Copyright © 1975, Carol Muske
All rights reserved
Feffer and Simons, Inc., London
Manufactured in the United States of America

Library of Congress Cataloging in Publication Data

Muske, Carol, birth date
  Camouflage

  (Pitt poetry series)
I. Title.
PS3563.U837C3   811'.5'4   74-26021
ISBN 0-8229-5259-9

Acknowledgment is made to the editors of the following publications for permission
to reprint certain poems in this book: *Antaeus, Eating the Menu: Poems 1970–74,
Elima, Esquire, Goddard Journal, The Little Magazine, Mundus Artium, The Nation,
New York Quarterly, Rapport,* and *Tenth Muse.*

"Swansong" is reprinted by permission of Esquire Magazine, © 1974 by Esquire, Inc.
"January" first appeared in *The Little Magazine.* Copyright © 1974, The Little
Magazine.

The publication of this book is supported by a grant from the National Endowment for the Arts in Washington, D.C., a Federal agency.

For my mother and father

For Daniel

and . . .

For Edward

unless I go in a mask

How shall I know myself among my faces?

—W. S. Merwin

CONTENTS

I   *Voices*
  Hot Springs   3
  Scarecrow   4
  The Visitor   6
  Traveling   7
  Voices   9
  Child with Six Fingers   10
  Birth   11
  Rendezvous with a Harp   12
  Swansong   13
  Next Time   14
  Luetta   16
  Old Movies in New Delhi   17
  Rice   18

II   *Camouflage*
  Camouflage   21
  Hyena   22
  Rite   23
  Concertina   24
  Photographer   25
  Mercenaries   26
  Lie   30
  The Goodyear Blimp as a Force in American Poetry   32
  Talk Show   33
  The Trance Artist   34

III   *Ice*
  Freezing to Death   39
  January   40
  Found   41
  At Yoga Class   42

IV   *Salad Days*
  Salad Days: Nebraska, 1964   47

VOICES

HOT SPRINGS

for Meg

Well she said like this
water from taps whose roots
go down to the old stove
come up in a stone mouth
a red storm that passed once
left its heart under a stone

Below it is autumn
heat from the flood
each wrist a reed filling
on a slope

I sink twice into my innocence
deep in the caldron
I lose skins
swim she says
it's easy

SCARECROW

It seems your dreams cost something
the crows kept track
of how you spent your nights
last summer
and are here to brief us

with your permission they will create
a past for you
give it arms and legs
a voice
to tell us everything

are you listening closely?
do you have anything to say at this time?
we have the tatters from your mattress
we have matches
and hair from your son's hobbyhorse

we have a candle and a woman's gold watch
are you listening closely?
we have evidence against you

we have the orange skins
we have the photographs taken by the sea
we have the photographs taken in bed

listen closely
we have the lost theater tickets

we convict you
of the woman's gold watch
of your son's hobbyhorse
of the orange skins
and the photographs of candles

there is no mercy in this court
the crows will please remove the evidence
there is no mercy
the crows will remove the theater tickets

listen now
we will create a present

THE VISITOR

At night the ghost comes round to visit her,
waits till her husband turns in the bed,
roars off down his old soft tunnel
calling mother.

The little light from the window
shines through his eyelids.
She smiles, her hand fishing in the mirror
for a light.

He nods and sits.
The mattress creaks.
They listen, asking little of each other.
An hour. Two.
A hitch in the moon's smooth rhythm.

She smokes, laying her dreams out
on the quilt.
He nods again, recognizing old friends:
the tree, the lamb, the faceless queen.

When he leaves, she dreams easily of walrus.
Shuffling on splayed feet,
tusks drawn up,
they squat at her bedside
for hours,
then lead her speechless across tundra
to sunrise.

When she wakes, she washes her body.
Her husband eats eggs in the kitchen,
wondering at her lack of appetite,
the light in her eyes.

TRAVELING

for D.

All travelers come to separate frontiers.
—Adrienne Rich

I

Your travels go on without me.
Even the world turns resignedly
into its own shape
night after night
and loses track of you
sailing some unnamed strait,
making maps of your passion.

In these rooms above the city
I light dusk's plunder like props:
doll and sundial
Balinese stump—
all summoned and set
as sad edges
of this country you visit occasionally.

II

Traveling's a trick I never learned:
how to keep tame shapes in valises
and move into the size of the landscape.

How clever I thought myself
on my short trip
to the sun.
I might have known
the long woman in the alabaster bath
would sing in the one language
I failed in.
I left her on high C
a note of glass
in the glamorous tide.

Myself imagining
a glass express
a whistlestop in some clear country
beyond stamps or tongues—
beyond even your passing fancy.

III

Your fantasies absorb mine,
settle like clouds on my shoulders,
blue cumulus,
come home to me at night
spreading false rumors of sunrise.

I have stolen light, brother,
from a dim pinnacle of justice.
And your discarded maps are mine.

We start out separately
from the same point,
arrive at this uncharitable sunset.
When the moon rises with our eyes
you will tire.
I will suffer my own will—
an afterthought, a codicil,
old homing pigeon that keeps coming back
though I move from house to house.

Now the frontier's ahead
and we're blind,
visas denied.
Imagine dying
as an act of diplomacy,
a reminder as the hearthfire turns wild
how you once loved
going places.

VOICES

She broke faith with the ice cream sticks
the painted rocks unfashionably stacked
and the roots of glory
(a plant dried in light).

In her house the stones rolled,
sticks snapped
and she sat, unmoved, listening for the voice.

She rubbed gold
and the sea came into her telescope.
Three seedless beasts, jeweled as eunuchs,
set watch about her ankles.

In the afternoon, she went to church
through the trees. The bees
lay dazed in the honey,
exhausted by gold. Moss berries fell.

She threw the first ring into water,
the second into earth. In her own voice
she testified, crying: I owe nothing more.

Later, when she put her hands in dough,
she heard another voice—explicit, sexual.
It took her to the porch,
to the yard.
She walked quickly.
The little winds blew stars into her mouth.

CHILD WITH SIX FINGERS

for E.B.H.

I felt no pain when they cut it off
only a coldness like rain
on the edge of the hand
where it was
the ache came later

it grew crooked
its sense was different, sixth
a feel for passing shapes
edges, lips of bells or bark

sometimes I tied it with string
it sang to the thumb

I lean on trees now
feel the roughness with my shoulders
they gave me a ball
instead I watch birds fly
thinking of wings

BIRTH

My lust tastes of blood in this wild.
My lover lost,
his little crutch humbled
as the moon rose to summit.

I'd heard the ladies here
had a way to make it painless—
I see now the wind
in these unspeakable leaves
is a lie.

I've inherited an orchard of myrrh,
this huddled sunrise,
all mine for a kiss
and a minute of light.

Tell my lover
this is the place that waited for me
beyond impervious titles, his diamonds.
Keep in mind how we die,
how hyenas eat pain from the cradle
and cypress, unbridled, give birth
to something lost,
something tricked in the wind's clear pitch—
its bottomless circling.

RENDEZVOUS WITH A HARP

It was too big to take on the subway
so she came to it every day
that winter in the room
where it waited on one foot,
sly seabird.

She sat down and opened her hands,
parted the wings one by one
till it flew ahead of her fingers
singing
the lame foot skidding on gold.

The sun turned its back on the glass
and paled as she sat
obstinate
green-eyed
her foot on its foot
pumping.

The fire died.
Snow hissed at the window.
Above her head a baroque hailstorm
failed in 4/4 time. She sang,
unable to hold the bright hinge
to her heart.
Lame savior she sang.
The harp bowed as she left
and sat, chastened by scales,
wondering.

SWANSONG

for Rose

The late Miss H. came to us Wednesdays at four
direct from the steno pool.
We waited, twenty of us in toe shoes,
slumped against her basement barre.

She was big,
her white hair bobbed,
her blue fox insurance against
ladies who called her déclassé.

Sometimes she told us how it was
when she danced *Les Sylphides*—
she, the ingénue with natural turnout,
withers drawn in the white light
of favored nations.
The Bolshoi sent its guns for her,
the heavy breathers from Minsk.
Miss H. leaped through their lines unruffled,
the season at her feet.
(Her lover Hans, a simple huntsman,
was at her side
the night in Dubrovnik
when a cab crushed her great toe.)

The swan died officially in St. Louis in '53
on a makeshift stage strewn with roses.
She gave her all,
then came to Minneapolis
where she taught us toe dance.

She often wept, sipping brandy,
nodding when the needle stuck
on a crack in *Romeo and Juliet*.
Those days we stood on ceremony:
mute sisters of the dance, we froze
holding second position till six
when the mothers came.

NEXT TIME

for Ellen

This time when I get out, I'm going to get back to everyone who
wouldn't let me be me, and show them all who I've become.
—E.L., Women's House of D., 1972

I

In this one
I go into their churches
pick the shadows from the lock
and move my light into heaven

Jesus stands back
his gang of angels
with brass chains
stand back

and see me
take my time
pluck the sweet tongue of Satan
from its cradle
hold up his holy air
for nickels

my hand in the poorbox is proof
I take only what belongs to me

II

The store sits pretty on the block
the manager's eyes shine prices
his signs invite me
I roll in on a steel carpet
as cold rolls out

inside the legs on hooks
the fingers in bags
snap to my rhythm
I put my knife in the butcher's side
say please your red meat
his smile drops to the scale
weighing nothing

III

I push in a skylight
drop eight feet into the dining room
where they're eating meat with silver
sipping wine and toasting their sense of taste
I ask them for what they can spare
they give me money

IV

I walk away from this
as far as I can
away from it
and it follows me
wherever I go

it comes like my last step
running
when I walk slow
it knows how to wait
it listens as I tell them
again and again
I'm a good person

LUETTA

In her cell
she puts things in order:
sink bed chair.
Three walls are stone,
the fourth, made of iron,
moves.

In six months, no sun to touch
her skin. She works the laundry,
feeds sheets into mouths of heat,
drops an ironing board
and bends
pressing hearts to the flat.

At midday she folds muslin and croons,
her voice filling noon's dead drum.
Dark bird she sings dark bird.

At night she holds a reed clean with her tongue,
plucks up a moon, a river.
She leans, a sweet convenience. . . .

Her mother's letter comes full of down-home medicine:
I believe without sun
the skin gets
thinner.

OLD MOVIES IN NEW DELHI

She sits cross-legged,
a peach drops in the garden.

She lays her goods on light—
like a mirror face down on water
waits to see what fish will catch
on pure reflection.

Choose she says.
I pick ankle bells and amber beads,
pleased by plunder of other lives
I might have lived,
a jewel in Krishna's eye
surviving luck
and touch.

She spits.
Bargains shrivel in her fists.
She turns the mirror face up

to fate, my own face hung
in the ancient tree
she came from—
Shiva selling trinkets
and lies.

Mother, I make a pact
with the monkey god:
for his absence
my abstention.

He will give me back my face
and I will give him his—
a fair trade
as living goes.

RICE

Their calendars are based on rice.
During drought, the days repeat—
the hours huddle like crows,
wait in lines
for dusk to grow light again.
The people walk in their sleep
to the New Year, an identical dawn
when fish move in threes. A sign of rain.

The monsoon is near.
When the rains come,
knives hang in trees.
They glitter.
A sail passes on the river.

When it pours, the rice is cut free.
It swims east to the river.

What is eaten by fish endures,
turns to weed and sleeps.
What escapes flies in threes to another weather.

What is washed up becomes a ghost,
haunts the paddies at dawn
wearing the masks of the starving.

Next season the children draw in dust
and tell riddles:
What day comes twice?
Day without rice.

CAMOUFLAGE

We assume different colors
to look the same,
saying how pleasant, not stirring.
The hunter, of course, wears red.
He stalks
unamused by small talk.

He knows the bone.
Confers under moons with skeletons
discovering at dawn
the solution.

For us it is ability
to wait with rocks and leaves,
barely breathing.
To understand water,
its different depths.
To feel duplicity in everything

       stones with eyes
       weeds that breathe and suffer.

What I am speaking of
is possibility: trout
moving through tea leaves,
white rabbits flying in snow.

When the hunter turns his back on the moon
he is deaf,
running against himself.

In this dark season
I have grown a rough coat for winter,
feel my hand budding with hardware,
my sweet smile
moving through stone
like a new species.

HYENA

She finds grief, her meat,
on a plateau
full of the moon's ammunition.
Her cousins follow, lift eyes
wide as torches
in the storm rock.
Dream birds lengthen
like wounds in the sky.

The shadow's task is primitive:
to sense doom and follow it.
She comes each distance to death
and eats what light is left.

It is her laughter on the slopes
at night.

RITE

To be purist was to go up alone against gravity
like salmon, dumb
covered with a substance like honey
choking on the bone of proof

It would be by accident when it came
casual treason
a fever of religious plants, roots of baptism
moving earth

To repeat trancelike the impossible
combinations of numbers
or words like
                eucalyptus
                cobalt

Come upon us
                disaster
                killer tides
all manner of bees
seeking death head-on
                      in our eyes

CONCERTINA

after Ghalib

The air is filled with unfriendly music.
In the street, I am confronted by three angry instruments:
a mandolin and two furious cellos.
They are fed up with my indifference,
this preoccupation with my own dissonance.
They shriek and pluck the strings across their hearts
                            in attitudes of despair.

Later they invite me for sherry in a bordello
and try to reason with me,
weeping white gloves, noting repeatedly my resemblance
to a harpsichord. I spy an old whore
across the room, staring at herself in an hourglass,
humming patriotic ballads.
They say she collects
hearing aids from dead soldiers,
listening to them at night
for clues to human behavior.

In my palm she sees a long voyage
into a tall dark piano.
She kneels and kisses my ears.
The music begins to drive me mad.

I take her advice
and leave by a side door
pursued by the sound of flutes.

PHOTOGRAPHER

Light has limits. What he can't see
he believes in. He tacks up background.
Shadows explode from the flash,
winter trees, victims.

Noon comes to find him
at home in the color blue,
whistling in a minor key.
In his dark room
he seeks clarity—
turns to acid
in unmarked bottles.

Light in the abstract bores him.
His shapes labor against light,
make gestures in space like mimes.

At midnight he puzzles what presence eludes him.
The space between trees,
the moon's other side.
Eclipse spins from his thumb.
Sunrise. Sunset.
He can never get it right.

M E R C E N A R I E S

*Diplomatic Relations Severed Between
Individual Interests and Major Powers
—from a newspaper*

Diplomatic Relations

Your words are native to some pale country
that sold itself
war after war
to any enemy with money.

Your words are tired
that have lied in every language
for a hireling's death.

I would be surprised
to find them at home
in this valley of orphaned fortitude.
I would be surprised
to find you on fire.

Severed

I had the film developed today.
I visited the bombed-out villages with the stills
but no one seemed interested.
I no longer believe in your suffering
or mine.
I believe only in the fire now—
the fire
and the absence of trial
before burning.

Between

Pay us for what we were hired to do.
Pay us our wages and we will kill
with an ease that amazes.

You misunderstand our labored passion—
we are called "plague"
as we gather
your tired brides
to our breast.

We seek sanctuary in these sad abbeys
at sunset.
Drunk, with guns we make our amends:
sing your bad anthem,
shoot echoes from the old bells
with bullets
round after round
till the white flag of dawn comes crawling,
till your sullen streets join us
and sing.

Individual Interests

Your mother has snubbed me.
I saw her at dawn
lugging her cornucopia of radishes and dung
along the Zuider Zee.
She stared beyond me
as I spoke.
I have spent the morning pondering
what has placed me
in her disfavor.

All my comrades are war orphans
gathered like shocks
into this rotting barn of a country.
They demand passion like yours,
they hunger for the sweet embrace of the occupied.

(Remember how we fell so slowly through the light
into the wide berth
of slackened grass
and I believe I sucked you dry?)
My pilot, my war hero,
you guided us home through the stars.

If your mother comes seeking me
I would caution her: old woman,
do not fear this ammunition belt, his beard—
but wear lace and your poor fake tiara.

How can I make her believe
I want no one's blood,
only certain hostages of the senses
who will desire me as I am—
a paid survivor
who will kiss my wounds
and pay me, love,
my due,
my king's ransom of screams.

and Major Powers

1

In the half-light I put on lipstick,
paint wings around my eyes
and go outside
to find politeness in a Chinese restaurant,
to drink as the radio reports come in
and the fire rises in the jaws of the beast
between us.

2

What we have in common keeps us separate.
They will buy your death, your irony.
The shadows inside us move easily to ruin.

3

I have no children
I search slick magazines
for orphans I would like to own

4

There is a fire beneath the floorboards
Tell her to walk in her new high heels
Tell her to smile

5

They were quarreling in the next room
and one of them
I think it was *her*
made so much sense to me

LIE

A lie is told
in the course of a conversation.
The liar lies,
his eyes grow wide, then sly.
His mouth operates like an oven:
out pops a blond loaf of bread.

The liar's face is troubled
with the unflourished truth—
his money is dying,
pine forests are bought up by fat men
who cheat at chess,
something his mother once said
does not impress his creditors.

He has only this last vanity:
a philanthropy of tin
from which he pieces together
his symbol, his distance.

His habit in sleep
is dreaming a listener's face
mottled like clay—
he touches and smoothes away the bad rumors.

Asleep his lies command respect in major cities.
He never tires of the finale:
himself in a stubbled field at sunset,
a background punctuated by his followers' cries
as he lays hands on the little ones,
the innocents.

In this scene he is invincible
in leather fringe—
he touches their cornsilk hair,
their little round skulls,
conjuring love and peace,
praising the truth—
how it saves,
makes everything
all right again.

THE GOODYEAR BLIMP
AS A FORCE IN AMERICAN POETRY

It floats there
remote as some June day in '56
you slammed the screen door
and it bumped up
on the sleazy weather of your wet dreams—
number one of the great old hits
made famous that season
in the basement.

He said in his poem:
"at best a silver blowfish
flung in the toppled white tide."
Dressed to the nines
it winced as it heard this.
It didn't like riding in the sidecar
or the service elevator.
It had no ivory tusk
or coat of arms.

That summer you went to the gas chamber
again and again
in search of the same total shine
it gave off in its martyr heaven:
"at best a bloated notion of grace,
a lust so pure, unencumbered by love."
Pale, balding,
you smoke cigars now and then
and remember.

TALK SHOW

Our host was a diamond stickpin,
a star,
and I sat on his couch all night
recalling my childhood.
The kliegs leaned for me,
as I sunned
under the illusion of height.

Our host bowed his head
admitting that there was an Asia,
that death was a fact for us.
I forgave Hollywood its wars,
the perpetual monsoon.
I forgave our coroner
for the cockfights,
the miles of dead cypress,
and courted fame,
my face smiling away from my face.

Who said the host
are you?
and I smiled *my* smile
as the band played half time
and the word APPLAUSE rose
like a shrewd moon
over Mother Pacific.

THE TRANCE ARTIST

Discovered in the living room
at five or six
how one foot follows the other
quite naturally around.

Recalling how far away
I heard her
chopping dill on pine.
The lamplight fixed
the flowered rug in place.
I turned and turned
and outside
snow came stuttering in the air.

Records whistled from their sheaths
and soon the Zenith breathed Strauss.
My eyes set
on the painted snake,
the needle-arm that nipped the plate
and ground out waltzes.

The twelfth time round
I let the heroes in.
On snowy wings they swept me up
and flew off
to favored places,
where I stood by like the moon,
benign, unrivaled,
spinning on the meager axle of necessity.

I turned in time
to grander exploits,
not mine
but part of other, gaudy lives
that drew me

from some dim-lit periphery
to light.

On Tuesdays I wore shoes
with lead moons nailed on
and danced half time on sawdust.
But here I was inspired to any task
they asked of me:
wingfoot
I eclipsed myself.

Sun and stars,
the planet's harp was tuned
to my bright heels.
I never stumbled once—
the clumsy Muse who could not step
to other borrowed Springs.

My mother called,
I glided in
and plucked the snake
who nodded once
and dropped in place,
his smile conspiratorial.

Later I ate herring
with my brothers
and watched the snow rise
inch by inch
outside the window.

FREEZING TO DEATH

I

The bedclothes grow stiff around my body.
The pitcher cracks. Light comes,
losing heat. I sit blowing ghosts into my wrists
nursing old skepticism.

Getting out of bed
I step into a drift.
It is falling everywhere now—
into my shoes, the vases,
the baskets of painted cherries.

II

My body moves bladelike through mirrors.
My head turns, a spool winding down
the last great ring of bone at the throat.
Cape of quartz. It snaps
light along the spaces of my spine,
pressing speechless against the marrow—
dead thumbs on a buzzer.

III

Who breaks my little imprints into salt?
Sparrow tracks. A new brightness
rises in my lungs.
When I open my mouth
it comes out in a stream.
Skinless. Circuit of stars.

IV

I've scratched a message on an icicle.
My palm rests on the table,
a snowstorm in progress beneath it.
My thumbs itch.
My left heel burns.
They say you don't feel a thing.

JANUARY

Her breath growing dim,
and some other kind of sleep
hitching her scalp in
a little nearer to death,
hook in spine,
she rides the killer's wake
as he trolls
the open water.

January's no time to die
says the priest.
The window hoards light
and we freeze in the lake.
Sleep till the thaw
and mud forms tunnels
or softer graves.
She hears him call down
darkness
as he leans by the bed
where she swims.

Later she will fly,
her wings fold under
as she lies on used beds
in the month of no color.

Frog and bear stunned in their own fat
slumber,
the month hardens into ice,
and she floats alone,
her eye on the rapids.

F O U N D

for M.S.H.

There was an ancient Spring inside the glacier
explorers tapped it
took tin dippers and drank

It melted and goats came out
children thin with cold
blue-eyed

Roses of sage pressed against the underlip of ice
birds turned on wires

The children gathered in twos and threes
followed the long weeping
to the edge of the floe
and stood calling back
across the water

AT YOGA CLASS

for Jeanette—and Paul Gorman

The leaves breathe outside a glass house
made of panes that fold and separate
like petals.
The master sits inside,
his body folded
in the form of a flower.

In the room next to the room of glass
a woman takes off her dovecolored trousers,
her silk blouse
and the heavy rings from her fingers.
She lets her hair hang
between the bones of her back,
places her cigarette in the pearl circle of an ashtray.

She enters the room of glass
as skin
and the hair that rises like tendrils of breath
between her legs.
The screen between the rooms shudders as she passes,
its bloodcolored trees tremble and bend into pools of black.

She sits with eleven others,
her ankles bent beneath the hard points of her hips.
They breathe:
the twelve students
the master
the leaves outside the window
the screen like the partition between heart and bone—
bellows pushing out the dark wind.

A small movement of smoke
circles above the woman
whose life is made of ashes.
She breathes with the others,
their mouths eating the air
in the exact fashion of fish,
the lungs working like looms
to weave a fabric smooth and new
as the respiration of sleep.

When the smoke makes a tree
and folds them in its branches
they go on breathing
their eyes cool
their fingers hung at their hips like fringe.

In the heart of the flame
they sit still, conspiring,
watching the tree
and the worlds of the screen silently collide.

She smiles,
all thoughts gone from her body
from her body's lust and willfulness
its capacity for hatred, for anger
its dim nipples and hair
its green eyes gone gray
above her own mouth breathing
length after length
of the innocent, murderous air.

IV   SALAD DAYS

SALAD DAYS: NEBRASKA, 1964

for John T.

I

On the plane
that doubled as crop duster,
hunching with the drunken pilot,
I watched the land
run jackrabbit
for miles,
ragged as our own small flight
from the dull imperative of sky.

Under us rolled
the casual gravity of Nebraska
sulking in our shadow,
sucking in its fringed lip of cloud.
Me and the '64 flight-school ace
heading downwind in a Cessna.

Out on the airstrip
signals ignite,
the feedbag full of butterflies
explodes in the opposite direction.
The tower woos us with radar
but we slip under its net,
turn due west to the panhandle,
and bend to the landscape,
pollen dropping from the wings.
Our target: summer, its unidentified harvest
blowing gold dust through the loam.

Out there, twenty thousand acres
roll back and draw our fire:
he tips the joystick—
we dive.

II

the angel drinking gin rickeys
alone on the drafty dance-floor
ruining her one silk dress
in the dark
I called Janie
as I came to claim her
in time for curfew

so late we were skating back
over the ice on the campus path
truant
her head against mine
against the sad platinum moon
the sure shine of her broad teeth
as she kissed me
and called me Tommy
her ginbreath a pale blossom in the cold

a rose
she pinned to the white wings of her hair
in the wind
cracking her patent-leather flats
in the rough spots
she rubbed with vaseline

the angel humming cha cha cha
through the unprecedented snowfall
of that year
she flew through the windshield
and they plowed the water-marked silk
and the blonde hair
under the rich soil
for good

on Saturdays
I waited there where the angel lay
thinking how they hated us

III

I knew a priest
a botanist
who kept his garden on the sly,
a plot that paid him
okra, kale,
mild heresies of fruit.

Each May he dug its dark currency
scattered seeds
pleased that nothing too extravagant
came up.

On the dusky garden tiles
we dreamed of vines, ruins,
grapes grown rife and eyeless
but everywhere his borders held
life's passion back.

This jesuit
who bled the fragile pulse of buds
and mimed surprise each year
to find a spider
in his seeds.

IV

John T., the doctor's son, loved horses.
A photograph taken at Ames shows us
neck and neck:
John T., me and the state fair stallion,
all of us
light-eyed, exhausted,
our breathing paced
to dreams of the grandstand,
the horseshoe of roses
dropped from heaven.

He was a thoroughbred,
full of a patient, irregular grace,
his neck held taut,
cheekbones faintly marked.
In the pale grass
his green eyes fired us
like ribbons he'd won
slumming in suburban derbys—
not steeplechase—
but barrel jumps and
dead man's canter.

He rode Pocoroncho
through his own nightmares,
riding heat to its center,
its dead heart lessened
by other pumping.

To stay the dreams of doctors
he rode away defiant—
the glide of his eyes,
a rhythm beneath the beat of hooves.

I knew how he'd fail
in the home stretch,
the doctor's son
who followed rodeo.
I knew who he was
when he gripped my mane
for the photo finish,
cried fly
          lady
               fly.

V

All spring that year
the storm of copper lilacs
imprisoned by screens
rubbed against each other
voiceless, discontent,
their plaintive smell
laying siege to my senses
as I sat under the orange lamp
reading Byron,

taking fond stock of my melancholy:
this one dead, a hero—
that one lying to me
night after night
on the princess phone,
a sweet wind through the screen
smelling of war and treachery. . . .

how the lilacs waved that spring,
purple cohorts
and the wolf prepared to come down slowly
on an old, suspicious fold.

VI

To prove God
is to deny him.
His quiddity a desperate scent
like the smell
the fox gives off,
cornered.

There is the pale argument of the afternoon
dying slightly on our hands.
To prove God
requires Aquinas and desire:
a failed momentum.

The window draws long spokes of sun
to its hub.
Ten thousand miles away
a man of God is consumed by fire,
flaming judgment of our penchant
for proof,
the iron logic of the curse:
to plead again and again
our argument,
turning the land to fiery
answers.

This year begins
the slow descent to Hell,
the Asian war,
the ghost crusade

and John T.
nodding at his desk
moves idle to a loss
more final than exile.
This war will claim him
waking, late
his eyes hold sun like syllogism.

To prove God
you must *be* him,
young and untried
stumbling drunk through the twilight wheat,
full of pheasants startled into blue,
roaring to a new failed moon
your prophecy
your life.

VII

What it means to be a mutant,
to force the cruelest truce to blossom:
that failed landscape exacting, at last,
compassion.

For a while we lay down
on the quick-moving earth.
It took us
untied like violet along the sunken river
at sunset

to where our own eyes
could find a little peace:
some green hem of the river,
unclean
but breathing.
The summer dusk instructive:
John T. and the angel,
their bodies, their eyes
final as desire.
And the sun for once incorruptible,
at pains to spare them waste—
God or winter,
the pale, reaped season impending.

Those salad days, those dusks,
when crops rose shoulder-high
and waited
green
deceived
for harvest.

PITT POETRY SERIES

Adonis, *The Blood of Adonis*
Jack Anderson, *The Invention of New Jersey*
Jon Anderson, *Death & Friends*
Jon Anderson, *In Sepia*
Jon Anderson, *Looking for Jonathan*
John Balaban, *After Our War*
Gerald W. Barrax, *Another Kind of Rain*
Michael Culross, *The Lost Heroes*
Fazıl Hüsnü Dağlarca, *Selected Poems*
James Den Boer, *Learning the Way*
James Den Boer, *Trying to Come Apart*
Norman Dubie, *Alehouse Sonnets*
Odysseus Elytis, *The Axion Esti*
John Engels, *The Homer Mitchell Place*
John Engels, *Signals from the Safety Coffin*
Abbie Huston Evans, *Collected Poems*
Brendan Galvin, *No Time for Good Reasons*
Gary Gildner, *Digging for Indians*
Gary Gildner, *First Practice*
Gary Gildner, *Nails*
Michael S. Harper, *Dear John, Dear Coltrane*
Michael S. Harper, *Song: I Want a Witness*
Samuel Hazo, *Blood Rights*
Samuel Hazo, *Once for the Last Bandit: New and Previous Poems*
Samuel Hazo, *Quartered*
Gwen Head, *Special Effects*
Shirley Kaufman, *The Floor Keeps Turning*
Shirley Kaufman, *Gold Country*
Abba Kovner, *A Canopy in the Desert*
Larry Levis, *Wrecking Crew*
Tom Lowenstein, tr., *Eskimo Poems from Canada and Greenland*
Archibald MacLeish, *The Great American Fourth of July Parade*
Judith Minty, *Lake Songs and Other Fears*
Carol Muske, *Camouflage*
Thomas Rabbitt, *Exile*
Belle Randall, *101 Different Ways of Playing Solitaire and Other Poems*
Ed Roberson, *When Thy King Is A Boy*
Dennis Scott, *Uncle Time*
Herbert Scott, *Disguises*
Richard Shelton, *Of All the Dirty Words*
Richard Shelton, *The Tattooed Desert*
David Steingass, *American Handbook*
David Steingass, *Body Compass*
Tomas Tranströmer, *Windows & Stones: Selected Poems*
Alberta T. Turner, *Learning to Count*
Marc Weber, *48 Small Poems*
David P. Young, *Sweating Out the Winter*